God Is In There

God Is In There

Recognizing God In All The Places God Is

By Wade Galt

Possibility Infinity Publishing

To God...

Thank you for being in me and around me.

These Ideas Work For Me...

I wouldn't call them beliefs because I'm not attached to them. I'm not ready to kill or die to prove I'm right or that someone else is wrong. This is not dogma, so there's no need for anyone to argue. I'm not suggesting I'm right or others are wrong. I may be incorrect. I'm not saying I hold the only truth, the ultimate truth, or even truth.

This book is a collection of ideas that feel true to me, that inspire me, and that work for me (based on what I can see in my life). I'd love to hear how these and other ideas work for you. I see this as a two-way learning relationship that we can both learn from. I'm not the teacher. You're not the student. We're just two people exploring ideas about the divine in hope of improving our lives and the world.

Please Accept My Humility and My Grandiosity

It is my only intention that this work brings you closer to peace, love, joy, happiness, and a greater connection with the divine. Please excuse my limitations as a writer as I attempt to do this. It is not my intention to make anyone feel wrong, uncomfortable, that they need to change, or feel anything other than fully loved, accepted and supported.

Please accept my grandiosity in wanting to address such a huge and important subject (and any apparent presumption that I'm right). Please also accept my humility in doing my best to make myself vulnerable by sharing something I think will make the world a better place. I honor all those people, organizations, religions, beliefs, rituals, and everything else that seeks to do the same,

At the same time, I remain excited, open-hearted and open-minded to seeing how we may grow, evolve, and change how we relate with the divine and each other to bring about even more peace, love, and happiness.

God Is In There

A young couple had their first children (twins actually), and they wanted to teach their children about divine love.

Each parent had been raised in a different religious tradition than the other, and they both learned a great deal about how much they were loved by God.

After years of discussing, they were still not able to choose which religious tradition to raise the children in, so they decided to try something different.

They both agreed that the most powerful lessons they learned about God all centered around how much God love them, accepted them, and cared for them.

They also came to discover that although they had been raised in different religious traditions, they both found the spirit of God was in the other.

This was not completely consistent with all they had been taught in their religious teachings, which made it difficult for them to decide if they should pass along their religious beliefs to their children.

Eventually they decided they would not teach the children differing religious traditions, (which both seemed to be accurate) since both religions disagreed on certain points and ideas which seemed fundamental to the religions' belief systems, rituals, and practices.

The parents decided to teach the children the most important lessons they learned from their two religious traditions, which interestingly were areas where the two religious traditions agreed.

They decided that in order to keep things simple, they would only teach the children one new lesson every year of the children's lives.

Then they would do their best to live out that lesson so their children could see how their actions demonstrated the conviction of their beliefs.

They both knew it would do no good to tell the children one thing and then do another.

They had both learned a long time ago that their lives were the greatest teachings they could give their children.

When their children were born,

they began to teach the first lesson.

We Love You Exactly As You Are.

All they wanted their children to know was that their parents loved them, as they are, so very much.

The parents had read that the best thing they could do for their children in their first year of life was to love the children unconditionally, so they did their very best to do just that.

The children got to feel their parents' love and their parents' presence almost all of the time.

The children grew up to be very confident and secure in themselves, and they began to start asserting themselves as individuals.

The children knew their parents loved them and felt very secure in their parents' presence, but they also experienced that sometimes their parents were not around.

There were also times when the parents were not feeling so loving, and sometimes they lost their patience with their children, so the children experienced that sometimes it did not feel like their parents loved them.

It was at this point that the parents taught their children the second lesson.

God Loves You …

Exactly As You Are…

All the Time…

No Matter What.

The children still did not have the ability to fully grasp the words their parents said, so the parents began to pray as a family daily.

They would all hold hands, close their eyes, and thank God for all the blessings in their lives.

They would ask for God's guidance, and they would all hug each other when they were done.

The parents did not know how to explain it, but somehow, the children seemed to become even more secure in themselves.

The children were not yet speaking, but somehow, they seemed to be getting the message that God loved them. The parents could not prove it or describe it, but the message appeared to be sinking in.

The children were calm, happy, and confident people when they were with their parents and when they were not.

When they children turned two,
the parents shared the next lesson.

This next teaching would become
the cornerstone for everything else
they learned from there forward.

The parents pointed at their children's hearts and told their children, "God Is In There!"

The children's eyes lit up as they heard their parents repeat the message, "God Is In There!"

The parents took their children's fingers and had the children point to their hearts, "God Is In There!"

The children were in awe of the thought. Not only did God love them completely, but God was also inside them. God was that close to them. God was always right there.

Whenever the children felt sad, scared, or unsure of themselves, the parents just pointed to the children's hearts and said, "God Is In There."

As the children grew, they became more and more comfortable with the idea that God was inside them. Their third birthday presented an opportunity for further learning.

For their third birthday, the parents gave the two children a gift for the two of them to share.

There were two children, but only one gift.

When the two children began to argue over who got to hold the gift, one of the children pushed the other away from the toy.

The parents shared with the children the new lesson.

"*God Is In There,*" they said, but this time they took one child's finger and had the child point at the other child's heart.

"*God Is In There,*" they repeated.

"Wow!" thought the children.

"God isn't only inside me.

God is in them, too.

God doesn't just love me.

God loves them, too."

Here the parents began the third part of the lesson that would be the basis for everything else.

Lesson 1 (God Loves Me) was a very comfortable and nurturing message to receive.

Lesson 2 (God Is In Me) was equally appealing and wonderful to hear and to learn.

Lesson 3 (God Is In Them) would be the most challenging lesson to fully understand and practice.

Each year the lesson expanded, and each year the children were invited and challenged to include someone else in the circle of those who God loves and dwells within.

When they were four, their parents took the children's fingers and pointed to the parent's hearts and said, "God Is In There."

This realization led the children to consider, for the first time, that these beings who had always been providing for them were also people and also God's precious creations.

When the children were five and began playing with other children more often, the parents taught the same lesson – "God Is In There."

The lesson made sharing much more necessary and desirable. The other person was loved by God, and the other person had God within them.

Sharing with the other person was like sharing with God – the same God who loved them so much.

Loving the other person was just like loving God – the same God who accepted them as they are.

Being kind to the other person was as natural as being kind to God — the same God who gave them life.

Over the years the children learned many such lessons, and they learned that God and God's creations were all around them.

They became more joyful and loving every time they made the connection that someone else was a part of the same divinely-created and divinely-loved family as them.

Eventually, they came to learn that the lesson extended further.

One day the children were being unkind to their dog and teasing the dog unnecessarily, and their parents said those familiar words, "God Is In There."

By this time, the children were much older, and they had the ability to reason for themselves and be clever as well.

One child challenged the idea by saying that it was "just a dog" and that it was not loved by God as they were.

One parent replied to the children, "Can you look into that loving dog's eyes and honestly tell me you think God is not in there?"

The other parent followed with another question, "Can you honestly look into your heart, where God is, and tell me you believe God did not create this dog with love just as God created you?"

The questions paralyzed the children as they realized their parents were accurate.

They knew they could no longer treat any animal unlovingly without knowing God was in there — the same God who loved them so much and who gave them life.

A similar lesson awaited the children when they were stomping on a bed of roses one day.

The parents observed their behavior and simply asked, "Do you think God is not in those beautiful flowers you are killing?"

The question hit home so powerfully that they didn't even bother to argue. They realized that God must be in the beautiful roses, just like God was inside them. From that point forward, they had a new respect for plants and trees.

One other similar lesson presented itself one day when the children each destroyed something of the other's. One child tore apart a painting by the other child, while the other child took revenge by smashing the other's favorite toy.

When their parents came into the room, they knew he parents would talk to them about being loving to one another, but they had no idea they would hear the familiar question on that day.

The mother asked, "Do you believe that God is not in the painting your brother made?" As she asked this, the sister could see the hurt look in the brother's eyes. Clearly, he had poured his heart and soul into the painting. He had put his most sacred energy, the God within him, into the creation. The sister apologized and hugged her brother.

Then the father questioned the brother, "Do you believe that God is not in your sister's doll? Do you really think that someone else did not put their heart and soul into this doll just as you put yours into your painting? Do you not think your sister has put her heart and soul into the doll?" As the father asked this, the brother realized the pain his sister experienced, so he apologized and hugged his sister.

The two became amazed by all the different places they saw that God was inside. This led them to be naturally aware of and gentle with other people, animals, plants, and things. It impacted all of their interactions and relationships.

Though they had never been taught any formal religious teachings or introduced to a single spiritual teacher or role model, they understood an insight that was at the core of virtually all spiritual and religious traditions.

It was at this point in their learning, when the children were 12 years old, and naturally curious, that the parents introduced their children to the religious traditions they were raised in. Eventually, they introduced their children to all the spiritual traditions they could find, so that their children could decide for themselves which — if any — was best for them.

After reading and learning about all the different traditions, the children found themselves very confused by all the different rituals, rules, and practices.

Each tradition seemed to have something wonderful about it that reflected what they first learned. At the same time, each tradition also seemed to have something less than wonderful that went exactly opposite to the core teaching they learned. Somewhere along the line, it always seemed to happen that some person, ritual or rule forgot that "God Is In There."

After a few years of studying the different traditions, the children decided to stick to the simplicity of the core lesson they first learned —

"God Is In There."

The parents, upon hearing of this, did their best to prepare their children for the next step. They shared, "We have told you all along 'God Is In There' as a way to help you understand that you are interacting with a piece of God."

When you love each other, you are loving a piece of God – the same God who loves you so much.

When you judge each other, you are judging a piece of God – the same God who accepts you as you are.

When you are unkind to each other, you are unkind to a piece of God — the same God who gave you life. Keep this in mind in all you do, and it will positively shape and guide your life forever.

As the children thought about what their parents said, many thoughts came to mind. Some thoughts (the ones where they remembered being unloving to others) bothered them, while others (thoughts of being loving to those around them) made them smile.

They began to realize that when they criticized another for being ugly, too fat, too thin, mean, nasty, dirty, or anything else, that they were criticizing a piece of God.

They remembered their parents saying, "What God sees as beautiful is much different than what you see as beautiful."

The parents would also ask, "Do you really think you are so brilliant and perfect as to criticize one of God's creations?"
The question was humbling.

"But what about those people who are mean and nasty?" one of the children asked one day.

"Are you ever mean or nasty?" the parents asked. "Do you think that stops God from loving you?"

"But some people are mean and nasty more often than we are," the child replied.

"And some are mean and nasty less often than you are," the father replied. "Are you really so self-centered as to think that God sets the bar of acceptance just low enough for you to be accepted, but high enough for those you think are below you to be rejected?"

The mother continued, "Have you found or met someone you think God did not create, does not love, does not accept or does not live in? Do you really think God only lives in some of us, but stays away from others? If that's the case, how do you know God is in you?"

"Anytime you love another, you love a piece of God and you connect with a piece of that same loving God. That's why it feels so good," the mother added.

"Anytime you reject another, you reject a piece of God and you disconnect with a piece of that same loving God. That's why it feels so bad," the father shared.

"We are all God's children and God's family, equally created and equally loved," they shared.

"When we love God, in ourselves or anywhere else, we are actually loving ourselves because God is in us and fully part of us," they said.

"*We are completely made up of God and God's energy. God is all knowing and all present. God is everywhere and in everything. Everything is created of God. Everything has 'Godness' or 'Goodness' in it. There is no other substance or energy in the universe that is not God.*"

"When we love and accept the Godness around us and in us, we love and accept ourselves (because we, too, are made up completely of Godness and nothing else)."

"When we hate and reject the Godness around us and in us, we hate and reject ourselves (because we, too, are made up completely of Godness and nothing else)."

"Godness is Goodness."

"Everything and everyone in the universe is made up of Godness."

"Everything and everyone in the universe is made up of Goodness."

"Nothing else exists."

"When we think something other than God exists, all our fears, insecurities, stories, dramas, myths, and everything else like that seem very real."

*"When we deny what is (God),
when we refuse to accept Godness
and Goodness for what it is,
we simply are inaccurate or unable
to see the truth."*

*"When we know that nothing other than God exists,
all our fears, insecurities, stories,
dramas, myths, and everything else
like that disappear."*

"And we are left with nothing but Godness and Goodness."

"And Goodness (God) knows,

that feels so great."

"God is not just 'in there',

God is 'out there' too. "

"God is everywhere and always."

"When we keep looking for where God is not, it becomes hard to see where God actually is."

"We only look for those things we believe we have lost."

"If we could just stop looking for God, we just might find God."

Hide and God Seek

God invited me to play hide and seek one day.

I counted to 100 and then I opened my eyes.

I couldn't believe how easy and fun the game was.

I saw God here and there and everywhere.

Everywhere I looked, there was God.

Just a week before, we played the same game, but I was never able to find God.

I really hated that game. I felt so bad.

*But today I found God everywhere,
and the game was so much fun.*

I asked God why it's not always fun like today.

*God said, "The most fun game in the world is peek-a-boo,
but I like to call it 'Hide and God Seek'.
The game is no fun if nobody ever disappears."*

"Is that why you hide?" I asked.

*"No," said God,
"That is why you choose not to see me!"*

Acknowledgments

Thank you God... for being everywhere. I know I recognize you sometimes and fail to see you at other times. Thank you for being patient with me and for loving me at every step in the journey.

My intention is that all who read this book, including myself, will experience the joy, bliss and fulfillment that come from seeing you everywhere – in ourselves, in others, in our world.

About the Author

Wade has led retreats and personal growth workshops, authored books on spirituality, personal growth, finance, parenting, business growth & more.

He has worked successfully as a life coach, 4-day work week mentor, organizational consultant, computer trainer, sales consultant, executive coach, speaker, mental health counselor, management consultant, software designer and programmer, author, business analyst, financial counselor, and in many other capacities.

Wade has a Bachelor's degree in Marketing and a Master's degree in Mental Health Counseling Psychology.

He lives happily with his wife and children.

His email address is wade@wadegalt.com .

Author Blog & Website

You may visit Wade's blog & website at www.wadegalt.com .

Also by Wade Galt

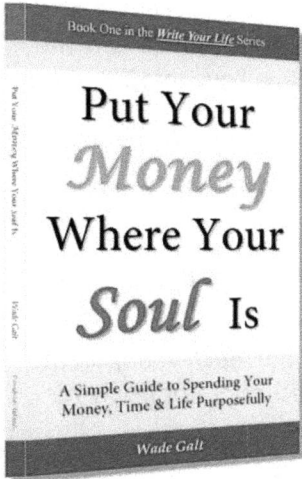

Put Your Money Where Your Soul Is

A Simple Guide to Spending Your
Money, Time and Life Purposefully

*Learn how to free up additional time,
money and energy by redefining your
relationships with money, time, people,
and things.*

*Simple strategies, exercises & tools help
you make powerful changes with very
little effort or struggle.*

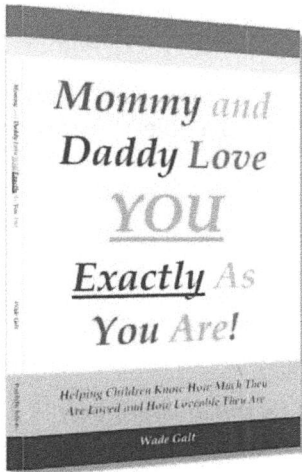

Mommy and Daddy Love You Exactly As You Are!

Helping Children Know How Much They
Are Loved and How Loveable They Are

My hope is that this book helps you...

*1) Let your child or children know how
special they are.*

*2) Remember how special your child or
children are.*

*3) Understand how much your parents
love(d) you, whether or not they ever
shared this with you.*

Mommy Loves You Exactly As You Are!

Helping Children Know How Much They Are Loved and How Loveable They Are

My hope is that this book helps you...

1) Let your child or children know how special they are.

2) Remember how special your child or children are.

3) Understand how much your parents love(d) you, whether or not they ever shared this with you.

Daddy Loves You Exactly As You Are!

Helping Children Know How Much They Are Loved and How Loveable They Are

My hope is that this book helps you...

1) Let your child or children know how special they are.

2) Remember how special your child or children are.

3) Understand how much your parents love(d) you, whether or not they ever shared this with you.

The *God Equals Love* Book Series

(Free eBook Versions Available for All Books)

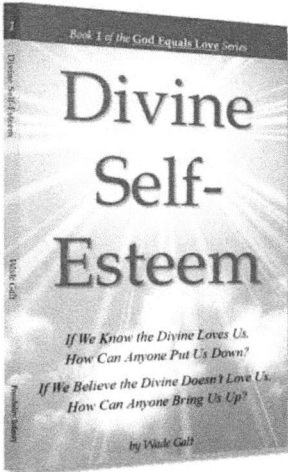

<u>Book 1 - Divine Self-Esteem</u>

Learning to Love Ourselves
the Way the Divine Loves Us

If we know the Divine loves us, how can anyone put us down?

If we believe the Divine doesn't love us, how can anyone bring us up?

Learn to see yourself through divinely loving eyes and catch a glimpse of the divinely-made miracle you are.

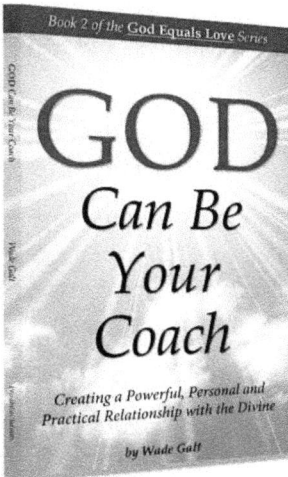

<u>Book 2 - GOD Can Be Your Coach</u>

Creating a Powerful, Personal and
Practical Relationship with the Divine

Create More Joy, Happiness, Love, Peace and Purpose in Your Life.

Learn One Simple Way to form a more powerful connection & relationship.

If You Knew You Could Connect with the Divine Anytime You Choose to Receive Guidance, Support, and Peace, Would You?

Will You?

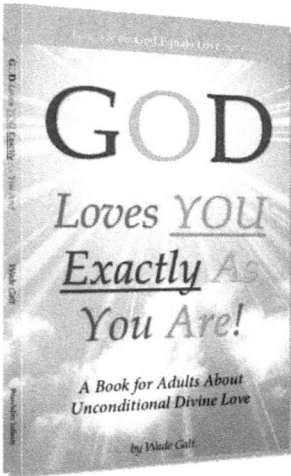

3 - GOD Loves You Exactly As You Are!

Understanding & Experiencing
Unconditional Divine Love

An Invitation to Consider & Experience the Life-Altering Understanding That You are Completely and Unconditionally Loved and Loveable EXACTLY AS YOU ARE!

What If God Loves You EXACTLY as You are?

How Would Understanding that Transform Your Life?

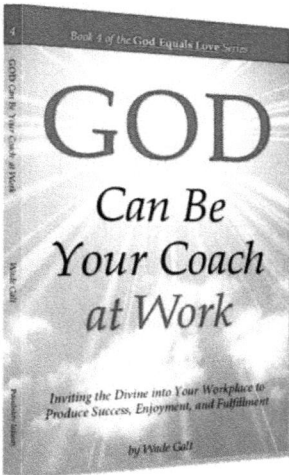

Book 4 - GOD Can Be Your Coach at Work

Inviting the Divine into Your Workplace to Produce Success, Enjoyment & Fulfillment

Few of us fully live our highest spiritual values in our workplace.

This is a source of frustration, shame, guilt & dissatisfaction for billions of us.

What if the divine actually wants us to experience life, love, joy, fulfillment, and abundance inside and outside our work?

What if the divine cares about our work simply because the divine cares for us?

This book is an invitation to work WITH the divine to create divinely inspired results for you and the world.

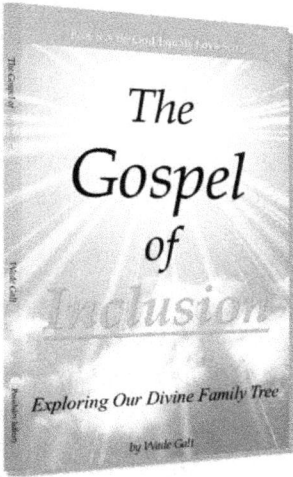

Book 5 - The Gospel of Inclusion

Exploring Our Divine Family Tree

Who is included in God's plan? Is it only people like me? Only people like you? What atrocities & apathy do we justify daily by declaring others are outside of God's chosen circle of people?

What if we really are part of one divine family? What would that mean? How would we have to change?

WARNING! Reading this book may lead you to (1) consider the possibility that we're all God's children and (2) do something about that. Proceed at your own risk!

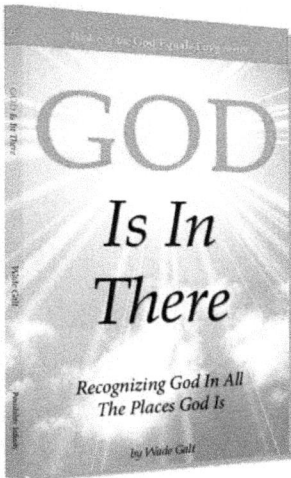

Book 6 - God Is In There

Recognizing God In All The Places God Is

If you could teach only one spiritual lesson, what would you teach?

What truth could you share that is so powerful, it would fundamentally transform the way others live?

There are a few core ideas that most spiritual traditions hold as true. Some believe that the most powerful and life-transforming truths are so self-evident and so obvious that all traditions agree about them.

This book contains one of those ideas.

7 - The Boy Who Wanted to Know God

The Story of One Boy Who Went from
  Knowing About God to Knowing God

*What would you be willing to do in
order to meet God?*

*Join a curious and excited young boy on
his journey to meeting the divine.*

You might meet God, too.

*The journey may be shorter and simpler
than you think.*

7 - The Girl Who Wanted to Know God

The Story of One Girl Who Went from
  Knowing About God to Knowing God

*What would you be willing to do in
order to meet God?*

*Join a curious and excited young girl on
her journey to meeting the divine.*

You might meet God, too.

*The journey may be shorter and simpler
than you think.*

Translated into Spanish (More to Come)

Autoestima Divina

Aprendiendo a Amarnos De la
Forma en que Dios nos Ama

*Si sabemos que el Divino nos ama,
¿cómo podemos sentirnos mal con
nosotros mismos?*

*Si creemos que el Divino no nos ama,
¿cómo podemos sentirnos bien con
nosotros mismos?*

*Aprender a verse a sí mismo a través de
los ojos de amor de Dios y echar un
vistazo a el milagro hecho de Dios-que
eres.*

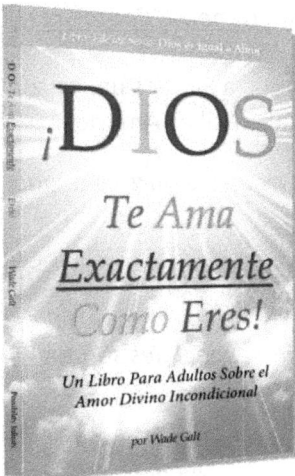

DIOS Te Ama Exactamente Como Eres

Un Libro Para Adultos Sobre el Amor
Divino Incondicional

*¿Y Si Dios te ama EXACTAMENTE como
eres? ¿De que manera ese entendimiento
transformaría tu vida?*

*Esto Es Una Simple Invitación... Para
Considerar y Experimentar... Un
Entendimiento de la Vida Alternativo...*

*Tú Eres Completa e Incondicionalmente...
Amado y Adorable... EXACTAMENTE
COMO ERES!*

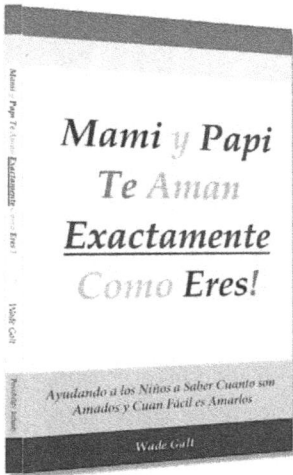

Mami y Papi Te Aman Exactamente Como Eres!

Ayudando a los Niños a Saber Cuanto son Amados y Cuan Fácil es Amarlos

Mi esperanza es que este libro te ayude a...

1) Hacer que tus niños sepan cuan especiales son.

2) Recordarte cuan especiales son tus niños.

3) Comprender cuanto te aman o te amaron tus padres ya sea que compartieran o no esto contigo.

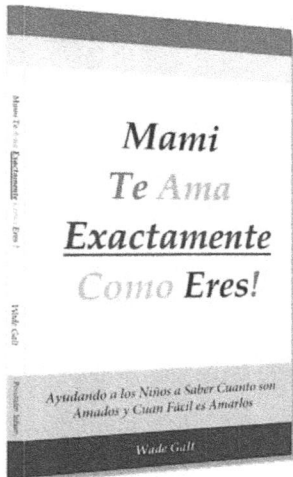

Mami Te Ama Exactamente Como Eres!

Ayudando a los Niños a Saber Cuanto son Amados y Cuan Fácil es Amarlos

Mi esperanza es que este libro te ayude a...

1) Hacer que tus niños sepan cuan especiales son.

2) Recordarte cuan especiales son tus niños.

3) Comprender cuanto te aman o te amaron tus padres ya sea que compartieran o no esto contigo.

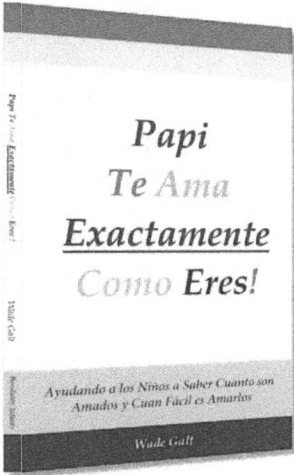

Papi Te Ama Exactamente Como Eres!

Ayudando a los Niños a Saber Cuanto son Amados y Cuan Fácil es Amarlos

Mi esperanza es que este libro te ayude a...

1) Hacer que tus niños sepan cuan especiales son.

2) Recordarte cuan especiales son tus niños.

3) Comprender cuanto te aman o te amaron tus padres ya sea que compartieran o no esto contigo.

To see these books and other books not listed here, visit www.wadegalt.com/books .

All profits from the sale of the GOD EQUALS LOVE books go to organizations and charities that seek to end unnecessary hunger and poverty.

New Book & Program Notifications

If you'd like to be emailed when we release new books, audios and other programs please visit www.wadegalt.com/notifiy to sign up for these notifications.

Share the Message & the Love

I hope this helps you see & feel how truly amazing and miraculous of a creation you are and how much the divine values you.

If you found the book to be helpful, would you please be so kind as to write a review on Amazon for the book or share the book on Facebook, Instagram, Twitter or other social media so others may know how it helped you?

Even if it's a super-short review, every little bit helps.

Thank you so much.

If there's anything I can do to help you further with this work, please email me at is <u>wade@wadegalt.com</u> .

All my best,

Wade

www.ingramcontent.com/pod-product-compliance
Lightning Source LLC
Chambersburg PA
CBHW070637030426
42337CB00020B/4056